Patiently In Wait

Donnamay Stewart

Bloomington, IN      Milton Keynes, UK

AuthorHouse™
1663 Liberty Drive, Suite 200
Bloomington, IN 47403
www.authorhouse.com
Phone: 1-800-839-8640

AuthorHouse™ UK Ltd.
500 Avebury Boulevard
Central Milton Keynes, MK9 2BE
www.authorhouse.co.uk
Phone: 08001974150

© 2006 Donnamay Stewart. All rights reserved.

No part of this book may be reproduced, stored in a retrieval system, or transmitted by any means without the written permission of the author.

First published by AuthorHouse 9/18/2006

ISBN: 1-4259-5633-5 (sc)
ISBN: 1-4259-5634-3 (dj)

Printed in the United States of America
Bloomington, Indiana

Table of Content

Nurturing	1
Just Like The Wind	2
Emotions Caught In The Storm	3
In The Midnight Hour	4
Can I Survive?	5
What Is The Definition Of Losing?	6
How Can I Say Sorry?	7
Conditions Of The Heart	8
Capturing My Soul	9
Falling Apart	10
Giving Yourself To Me	11
Tick Tock Goes The Clock	12
Waiting For Your Love	13
Worth It In The End	14
You Walked Out Of My Dreams	15
Does She Love You Like I Do?	16
The Last Day of the Year	17
Were You Thinking Of Me?	18
When Will This End?	19
Where Do I Go From Here?	20
You Walk With Me	21
Every Ounce Of Me	22
Is It About Me?	23
Leave Me	24
Let's Celebrate The New Year	25
To Be True Is To Be Free	26
Turning Of Time	27
All Games Aside	28
A New Start	29
I Need To See Clearly	30
I Hope You Experience Love	31
Is This Time For Our Final Goodbye?	32
I Wish I Could Stop Loving You	33
Sunday Morning	34
The Master Key	35

The Month Of June	36
What Do You Want From Me?	37
Why Does She Hurt You?	38
Wrong Timing	40
Are You Afraid Of My Love?	41
Let's Talk	42
Moonlight	43
Repossessed	44
Send The Elevator Down	45
You Bring Out The Best In Me	46
Hold My Hand	47
I Can't Settle	48
My Oasis	49
Destiny Will Unveil	50
I'm Ready	51
May Your Heart Rest	52
One Plant Of The Same Tree	53
The Blindfolds Of Love	54
The Body And The Heart	55
Too Busy	56
You Can't Walk Away Then Return To Play	57
Above The Clouds	58
One-Way Ticket	59
Friday Night	60
Physical Pain	61
When You're Feeling Down	62
Dining By The Water	63
Silence in the Stillness	64
Can Time Return?	65
Mellow Moments	66
Always Leave The Cage Open	67
This Love	68
Does Having My Heart Make You Feel Good?	69
Gentle Kisses	70
Reservations For Two	71
Each Step I Take	72
Healing	73

Power Of Agreement	74
Your Love Has A Hold On Me	75
Eighteen Years Old	76
Above and Beyond	77
Empathy	78
Time To Move On	79
Last Chance	80
I Will	81
Black Bird	82
Will Our Paths Cross Again?	83
From This Day On	84
Navy Lodge	85
A Ton Of Bricks	86
The Smiles Come So Naturally	87
The Valley	88
Power Of Freedom	89
Driving Down Memory Lane	90
Fulfilling Your Own Dream	91
Love Heals All Wounds	92
Memories	93
Mirror	94
Never Let Me Lose You	95
Relevant Authority	96
Wedding Day	97
Window Treatment	98
Young Love	99
A Woman In Love	100
Laughter	101
Reality	102
Broken Hearted Clown	103
Phenomenal Woman	104
China Cabinet	105
Coming In And Out Of Your Life	106
Encouraging Words	107
Everytime I Look At You	108
Girls Night Out	109
Hammock By The Sea	110

Hurt	111
I Did It My Way	112
Escaping The World	113
I Need You	114
Let Me Be Your Freedom	115
Let me off the Roller Coaster	116
Love At First Sight	117
Why Do I Feel Love Is A Lie?	118
Love Has No Price Tag	119
The Girls With The Frills	120
Love Is Like Building A House	121
No One Could Take Your Place	122
Pearl-the Rearest Gem	123
Speed Your Love To Me	124
Tell Me	125
The Attentiveness In Your Touch!	126
The Gift Of Loving Yourself!	127
There We Go Again	128
Self-Inflicted Pain	129
Climb Any Mountain	130
Two Ships Sailing In The Night!	131
Unconditional Love	132
Walking In The Rain	133
We Held It Together	134
My Personal Flight	135
The Act of Kindness	136
Wealth	137
What Is Poetry?	138
Rise And Fall To Expectations	139
Harnessing Family Values	140
A House Is Not A Home	141
A Thought For The Day	142
Butterfly	143
Humility	144
It's All About You	145
Let's Go Sailing	146
Like The Flowers Need The Rain	147

Love	148
Look Into My Eyes	149
Love Is Truly Being Able To Let Go!	150
Marriage	151
I Don't Want To Be An Obligation	152
No More Tears	153
Not Calling	154
Over The Rainbow	155
People Needing People	156
Possessing The Will Power To Live!	157
Sharing Is Caring	158
Shining Star	159
Son	160
Shattering of Trust	161
The Painting	162
The Valley	163
Not My Creation	164
The Zoo	165
Unity	166
Togetherness	167
One Plant Of The Same Tree	168

Nurturing

Nurturing is like motherly qualities that are hidden
deep within; waiting for the experience to arrive so
the qualities will no longer remain disguised.

Giving longing love to someone in need, bringing
them out to succeed. Tilting your hand in the outward
position, hoping they will respond and lend you the
same hand in future plan so you can continue to
help a man keep the cycle on a rotating plan.

Let's give each other the love that is needed
in order to succeed and pursue the nurturing
characteristics throughout the land.

Just Like The Wind

Just like the wind is what you are. I can feel you but
never is your appearance to me one that I can see.

I feel you in my spirit but like the wind you blow into
my thoughts, and never can I feel you in my arms.

I cannot reach out and touch the wind; not
being able to at times feels like a sin.

The feel of wind is ever so strong, making
the existence profound and long.

See, just like the wind is what you are,
leaving a fresh breeze upon my heart.

Emotions Caught In The Storm

I know you feel my thoughts rushing through the storm. I know if you could, you would be here for me to rely on.

Emotions are going pitter patter against the hearts of the two who have to be apart. Just like the patter of rain on the window pane, comes the patter in my heart, which longs for us to no longer be apart.

So in the storm, while the rain falls down from above, so is my heart waiting for only your love.

In The Midnight Hour

In the midnight hour when everything got sour, everyone
lost their power and we sat back bored stiff for hours.

Is there anything else to do in the midnight hour
when you're bored, but cannot sleep? I get out of
bed and land on my feet, praying the morning
would arrive and make sure the night I survived.
Mornings look so still and far away in this hour, but
the sun will rise again after the midnight hour.

Can I Survive?

Can I survive these weeks of torture; the answer
comes as yes, I will move about a little bit longer.

Survival instincts immediately come out whenever your
heart is ever in doubt. Your soul will forever dig deep from
under and come out shining above continuously to wonder.

Brush yourself off from all the dirt when you come
out, and ask for the grace to always be alert.

In the end you will see that a stronger person you will be.

What Is The Definition Of Losing?

How do you define loss? To some it's defined by material gains, which situations arise that caused them great pain. Losing your worldly treasures is simply a portion of what life has to measure.

To others who may have to give up someone close, which then truly doesn't leave you to boost.

Whatever you might perceive losing to be, just keep in mind having tranquility is the key. See this key will eventually open many doors that others could have seen, but purposely closed. Always remain to have peace in your heart, which will elevate you to a plateau with a brand new start.

How Can I Say Sorry?

I'd like to say sorry for the things I've
said, but oftentimes I am afraid.

Your feelings were hurt deeply by me, and from
emotional scars were left much debris.

Will you eventually accept an apology from me,
so in my spirit I can once again be free?

Conditions Of The Heart

The conditions of a heart that was making me fall
apart; the vigorous hurt brought about so much
pain, which lead the valves to bleed in vain.

Hold back the emotions one day, so your heart won't
experience the strain of falling in love all over again.

I have no reason to hold on any longer, so
with this in mind, I must let go of all the
emotions that once made me ponder.

The conditions of the heart is a sensitive matter, so I will
one day see keeping it under lock and key will prevent
me from getting this little heart battered with debris.

Capturing My Soul

Can you let go and set me free; by telling me to move on
with me—not living anymore in love rainbow strife?

Set me free once again I ask, giving me the chance that
I need to continue the path that is set aside for me.

My soul has been captured for oh *so* long. Only you
have the key that can open the door and set me free,
but are you willing to give up that part of me?

I need to know now and forever more, so the
rest of my soul can one day unfold.

Falling Apart

How can you say you don't love me anymore, when
our paths have traveled down the same road for so
many years, experiencing each other's tears?

I shared your dreams, watching them beam
in your eyes; holding them tight while they
made their existence into your life.

By your side I stood, giving you the support to stand
tall and carrying the family throughout the brawls.

My heart falls apart now, knowing how you feel. But I
have faith in love, so by all means I will set you free.

Just like the bird that soars I will let you fly, but you will
return home like the pigeon coming home in time to get
fed, because your heart is only being temporarily mislead

Giving Yourself To Me

I need to know if I will receive your love and yourself
you will give to me, so that I can set my soul free.

Holding on to my heart is a painful thing, so give
me back the key; I ask to unlock this heart and
I will then hope to have a fresh new start.

Only you can give me the key. Why can't you see that
you need to attend to me in order for my love to be free?

Release me now, I ask, so I can share this special love
that binds my heart with someone deserving of all these
things, and peace thereafter it will eventually bring.

Tick Tock Goes The Clock

The sound of the clock goes tick tock as I listen keenly and
watch my life on the emotional spot at twelve o'clock.

Between the hours, I listen to hear relief
blasting through the silence of my walls
making me see clearly once and for all.

Time stands still on the window pane of the love
hurting heart, waiting to gather love again.

While I wait the sound of the clock going tick tock you
anticipate, making it seem like a lifetime ahead, but in
reality you listen with hope and eagerness instead.

Waiting For Your Love

I only sit in vain waiting for your love all these years.
Now I must move on, because my patience is in vain
and it has caused me mental and heart strain.

You I love with no conditions from the start,
but your love I have to free to continue my
journey and to protect my heart.

I only told myself a lie when I thought I could give
my love to some other guy, but now I have to free my
soul to have the love I know I deserve forever more.

Give me back my heart, which you have captured.
Break the bond that chains me from giving myself
completely to someone. I need the key for my
soul, so my love I won't waste anymore!

Worth It In The End

This question I ask, hoping the answer is one that I
can depend on: Will this all be worth it in the end?

To start all over from scratch, making temporary
decisions that will one day last and ease your mind
to relax, hoping to fulfill your tedious task.

Did I make permanent changes to temporary
emotions that have me sailing on the sea of lost
devotions, or will things be worth it in the end?

To myself I ask these questions; leaving my
heart to listen to the message of the test in reply;
making me wonder at times am I living a lie.

You Walked Out Of My Dreams

Years ago you stepped out of my dreams, making things a
reality for oh so long and I stand alone to sing my song.

Every detail of my life you knew,
making this story ever true.

You were the one who showed me love and
made me feel what life's meaning was.

You alone saw all the qualities in me and
always wanted me to be set free.

Out of my dreams you walked and continuously became
the one true friend upon whom I could always depend.

This dream is ending now for me.
Oh baby, why can't you see?

Thank you for everything that you've done for me,
but now I suppose it's time to set you free.

Does She Love You Like I Do?

When you look at her, do you see me looking back?
Does she love you the way I have all these years, letting
you elevate to a world of your own, realizing that
love is free—not one waiting to bind you to me?

Does she love you in a gentle way every time you
are blue? Does she tenderly talk to you?

Do you feel love and see love when you are together, or are
you going through the motions on the sea of obligation,
feeling seasick inside while you continue to live your lie?

I know the answer to all these things because you
dream to me at night and I feel all your misery down
inside, so to me you can never continue to deny.

The Last Day of the Year

The last day of the year is a time for persons to
reflect on your life that was purposely spared.

This day for many is one to celebrate and party all
night long, but while doing this we must remember to
thank the almighty one for giving us the achievements
of the prior days; compelling to proceed toward
the end and making a quiescently descend.

The last day of the year for me is an extremely special one,
you see, because while watching others celebrate it gives
me the opportunity to sit back and meditate, knowing that
the end defines conclusion of a chapter that is now closed.

Then the New Year arrives, allowing me to engage
in another year of entertaining love from others, and
the ability to reciprocate while entering love's gate.

Were You Thinking Of Me?

Were you thinking of me when you called;
thereafter your fingers could no longer stall?

I didn't expect to hear from you, because I surrender my
heart to whatever must be, hoping the truth will set me free.

When two persons are whole heartedly connected,
then the bond is not easily affected.

For this reason I allow you the space, so you
can reflect without interference; making
your decisions wholly your own.

I know you think of me each day and night, even when
your phone calls are far from sight, so thanks for calling
to affirm the thoughts I know were true forevermore.

When Will This End?

Will this ever end? Our love to each other can one day
spree on the mountainous boundary of being free.

Free to be able to hold your hand; reassuring you that
I'm here for you to rely on, and that I can surely die on.

Can someone please tell me when this will end, so one
day we can completely see the reason why we were
meant to be from the very start when we first met?
When the connection was ever strong; defeating all
malicious plans, while we expressed true love to man.

I know I have your heart; even if we can't get
the fresh start that our love needs to bloom from
that single seed; while springing into fruition
and embracing each other into completion.

Where Do I Go From Here?

Where do I go from here? Do I stay and let my heart
play, or should I go away and allow my heart to stray?

From the emotions I can't hide, and certainly won't
deny, but can I continue to live in hope all day
long, while I hold on to my heart; giving myself to
no one at all, because all I do is ache for you.

Can you tell me where to go from here; to
never feel alone even when I'm amongst a
crowd? My heart cries out, aching aloud.

The final answer one day will come and then I will
surround my life amongst these plans, but until that day
arrives for me; I continue to be a woman waiting patiently.

You Walk With Me

Your spirit I feel in every step that I
take; this I know is no mistake.

You talk to me, you sleep with me, and your
love blankets and surrounds me.

You walk with me throughout my life, even
though our roads traveled separate paths.
I didn't need to ponder or even ask.

How can two people be so connected? One
would ask. I believe in destiny for my life,
and you have been the only one for me.

Every Ounce Of Me

There is nothing that I deny, when telling others of
the love I share. Every ounce of me wants to play and
express to you how much I truly cared all these years.

I share you, although I choose to be alone.

With every ounce of my fiber I need to explore
this heart's desire that I share forever more.

There is nothing left back for someone else, because
this girl belongs to you, which makes others turn
out to be fools, not being able to understand and
continuously treating me less than I am.

Is It About Me?

Is it about me, like you said, or will it
be a foolish game you play?

I know you feel the love inside your heart for me,
so can we now for once set ourselves free.

This is the only way it will be all about me;
not just words but actions I need.

Will it ever truly be one day all about me? You I
see and think of often times, but to myself true
love abiding in me I should never deny.

Oh can't I wait for the day when, like you said,
it will be about me, and your abundance of love
will pour out from within to set me free!

Leave Me

Why do you leave me and go away each time
your heart strays? Don't you see it prevents our
hearts from mending the severing of time, which
delays the process of you truly being mine?

Do you realize how you affect me with your actions
that aren't discreet? Just look into my eyes and you
will see exactly how much you're hurting me.

When you look into my eyes I know you see that love
resides here, so please stop the roller coaster rides and come
back to take my hand, so we can take the eternal ride,
which you know will last through all the emotional slides.

Never leave me again for another, my love, for
every direction you turn from here will get
you entrapped for selfish reasons and maybe
next time your heart will not be spared.

Your true love wants to see your heart soar, even if
from me you hide. I only need you to enjoy the ride.

Let's Celebrate The New Year

Come celebrate the New Year, by telling
me how much you truly care.

Stroll into my world, making things simply easy
to control. Then here you will stay to start your
New Year and forget all the previous cares.

Let us look back at the things that occurred in our
lives throughout the year, leaving our hearts without
care, and we will continue to give love a dare.

Come sit and converse with me all night;
while we watch the clock of time wind into
morn, celebrating each other until dawn.

To Be True Is To Be Free

Let yourself go by telling the truth to your
heart; allowing the truth to unfold in an
endless story for everyone to behold.

Set your spirit free by exuding the truth to me,
so your life will be an example for others to
see the richness that can be experienced.

Let us hold the door handle of the truth, opening the door,
which leads you into the abiding atmosphere of freedom!

Turning Of Time

The clock of time turns daily, but time is just a reflection
of your own mind; giving the opportunity to unwind.

Many don't heed to this experience, which forces
haste to set in; leaving much years of waste.

Rolling back the hands of time will give you the peace
and tranquility you need to persist; putting up the
bar that you need to resist the unnecessary deeds of
persons waiting to place the wool over your eyes.

This will make your vision very blurry, which postpones
your eternal gain due to the vigor and constant strain.

Take the time that you need to remember who
you are, and remember without anyone else you
were born, so ask yourself who is the star.

All Games Aside

Will you put all games aside; just to get
a moment to lie by my side?

All games aside is simply a wish, but we can anchor on
the sea of perpetual bliss, where in your midst I can find a
heritage of peace in abundance, feeling heavenly divine.

Will you put aside the board of games to utilize my
mental claims and soothe my emotional strains?

A New Start

A new start is what I need; being able to let go and
trying to bring out the inner beauty captured within.

I can only get this start, if you give me
back the only key to this heart.

You have possessed the key that will unlock
the divine purpose waiting for me.

Please, I beg, let me get this new start and cleanse
all the soul-binding relationships that have blinded
me for so many years, leaving me empty and full of
tears while I watch my life rotating to no end.

Tell me when you will give me that new start to
renew again my soul until the day I get old.

I Need To See Clearly

My eyes are like the freshwater pearls in the
sea, telling me everything that they see.

I can see clearly through these eyes and I need
no one else to continue with the lies.

I can see clearly when it comes to my heart,
because it has already been badly torn apart.

I can see clearly now I can say, because
love has made me this way.

Through crystal eyes is how I see, rolling
back all the wool;that blinds eyes and people
continually telling me a bunch of lies.

I Hope You Experience Love

I hope for your sake you will experience love someday,
because right now your heart is simply at play.

You will know the meaning of love when at night you
no longer can sleep; having endless thoughts of me.

You will experience love one day when you glance in
a mirror, and me you will see reflecting your way.

Love will enter the doorway of your heart when
I am gone, and from it, you will depart.

I hope you truly experience love some day, because
now you're captured in bondage while your soul
seeks for just one day of happiness to salvage.

Is This Time For Our Final Goodbye?

Your love has held me together for most of my life, but
now I must ask, is this our stage to now say goodbye?

You I will free for the sake of love; I
only want to see you sail on.

My goodbye will not last long—, just for a moment; I
only need to take your hand and give a piercing look
into your eyes, which will remain to give me my guide.

Let me know if this is our final stage, so
I won't feel any emotional rage.

You I will set free, but this time remember you can't
come back to me, because I will bind all the chains of
my heart, so I can truly receive a brand new start.

I might be able to learn the art of loving again,
if you guide me, being my one true friend.

I Wish I Could Stop Loving You

Why is my heart in still waters that will not move? I
wish I could just stop loving you, so I can find another
to whom I can be true; just as long as I stop loving you!

Your love has been like the sand by the sea
side that just stands still; swept smoothly until
another passes by to place footprints into that
sand that will remain a mark on the land.

If the water flows out of the sea to the width
of the footprints, then that is when they fade
away, but until then they're here to stay.

Sunday Morning

On this Sunday morning I write to the ocean so free; please
take my love to your depth and return it some day to me.

If even in another life I will see the wonders
of my heart exploring and be set free.

On the peaceful Sunday morning by the sea, my soul
finds tranquility for a while to capture my thoughts
once again and explore them fully with my pen.

I throw my message into the water, leaving no signs
for anyone to see, but only between the ocean and
me my heart's desires will reside, which bring peace
to my soul while I write by the ocean side.

The Master Key

You hold the master key; the only one made to
set me free, so can you return this original back
to me one day, so only on my love I will stay?

The date on my safety box will have to expire, leaving
no renewal for me, so this key you must return so
I can give you back your life's total refund.

The master key always possesses one owner. Duplications
you will never find, because the source has been
abolished and from copies will always hide.

This key is like pure gold, because when released
it captured the soul and like the brilliance of
the metal it shines to an everlasting level.

Will you return this key to me again? I ask, so
our love can evolve to a new dimension; waking
up tomorrow to a world of no more sorrow, and
love will be yours to keep; no need to borrow.

The Month Of June

The month of June didn't come too soon, but this was when
my heart returned home to you, sometime in the afternoon.

That was a significant month for me, because
once again the emotions were free.

The one I love, I finally got to see, making my heart wonder
in the thought of ponder, how could this coincidence be
real? The one I love I again can feel and glance into his
eyes for focus and a chance for renewal of strength.

June will be an unforgettable month, for memories
that were stored are valued as collectibles.

These memories will share a space in my
life and from me they won't depart, because
they are buried deep within my heart.

What Do You Want From Me?

Am I silly for wanting to wait, just to see
exactly what you want from me?

How do I prove my love to you that never did end,
but your mind was so confused because you looked
at me and thought you were the one to loose?

I only gave you back your life, so you could be
free to do the things that were meant to be.

Walking away took all of my strength, and my
heart all these years I tried so hard to mend.

Just tell me what you expect and this girl will do her very
best to prove again my love can conquer any test. My
love has always remained and in a still place it will stay.

What do you want from me? I know it can't be for
my love to stay and just wither away, while I look on
your life taking the long painful road that has no
end; until you realize once again that your heart was
always mine, so baby you're only wasting your time!

Why Does She Hurt You?

Many people don't find love in a lifetime,
so why does she continue with the pain that
gives you constant emotions and strain.

Why does she cage your heart to chain you to
her side, and not free you to be the person you
are, giving love to those near and far.

Does she think that this will last; making you
her puppet to string you along to a world that
only binds you to want to do wrong?

Does she hold you so tight, making your space to breathe
very limited; just to her alone she expects you to give; not
giving of yourself to the world, because what you have needs
to be shared, so people can truly see how much you care.

Why does she hurt you with physical pain,
doesn't she see what she has gained?

Her actions only tell me that she is weak, and your love
she will forever seek; trying to bind you to her feet.

She doesn't need to restrain you anymore, because
her love is selfish and has become a bore.

It must be sad sitting in her show, knowing she did
things to capture a man that truly belongs to another.
How long does she think she can continue this game,
holding things over your head to stay? Please tell

her those are all foolish games, will end up giving
her nothing but strain, which leads to zero gain.

Wrong Timing

Timing in life means a lot to me, and with this
time that was given to me, I will use properly.

My time I will take to reflect on the few mistakes
and be thankful that they were few, so I still have
the opportunity to make things up to you.

Everything in life has a schedule, which
at times controls life's module.

Once time is gone, it can never return. No one can change
the hand of time, but we simply use the quality time given
to provide the necessary transition to a tranquil position.

Are You Afraid Of My Love?

Fear is only false evidence appearing real. Is this
what you feel, and do you see this in me?

Do you fear the feeling you share, or is it the
need to succeed that upon you shall feed; needing
only to these feelings that you heed?

My love doesn't require much from you; just
the respect that I know is due. So simply step
up to the plate and stop allowing your heart to
hesitate, while your one true love has to wait!

Let's Talk

Come talk to me for a while; escaping the world just
for a day, so your mind can take a journey of depth;
leaving your imagination of soul that has wept.

Sit down and tell me your thought; no one will expose
your doubts inside, instead I'm here to protect and
from harm; make sure your heart does hide.

Let's talk for hours until your thoughts are clear, so you can
listen to inner thoughts, and your feelings you shall hear.

Talk to me I ask; stop wearing your disguisable
mask, which I see each time. You try tediously to
convince me that you're fine, but in your eyes I see
the sign; telling me you're longing for a little peace
of mind and some tranquility you need to find.

Moonlight

Moonlight, oh how bright is your existence,
illuminating throughout the night.

Shining from up above, your light reflects so much
vibrancy of love. With each shape that you take, you
filter through the dark, showing the earth that there
is a greater man; who places you over the land.

You share with the universe each night, shining
on and giving us a piece of your light.

Moonlight, I will watch you all night, because
there is a melody in each glow, which nightly
leaves a smile on my face that shows.

Repossessed

When your things are repossessed, this brings
about a feeling of making you feel less.

Situations arise in life that comes to create
difficulty and strife, but people outside looking
in would never imagine the humility this brings
to watch someone repossess your things.

This shouldn't come to judge your character, but instead
it builds your strength to become stronger, allowing
one to stand up and fight the ever going battle of life.

I know to many this is a job, but people at
times fall into situations beyond their control,
which leaves them to battle for their souls.

Letting go of personal belongings that you hold dear is the
ultimate test, but eventually you become eternally blessed.

Send The Elevator Down

Many ascend to the top, but when arriving at the
top of your journey, the most profound story is to
remember to send the elevator back down; that
others may change their lives and come around.

The journey to the top, for so many seems far away;
instead sharing and caring takes time away from
the short-term vision where selfishness abides.

Give others the opportunity to join you on
your ride. So send the elevator down to let
someone experience a joyous glide.

You Bring Out The Best In Me

Looking back on the calendar of time, you reflect once
again in my mind, reminding me of all the positive
things and explosive emotions being around you brings.

You bring out the best in me, and anyone who
knows can clearly see that your love embraces
me with a depth no other has found.

How many times have we tried to escape the
roller coaster ride, but time won't stop to let either
one of us off, so for this reason our love won't
remain a past; instead it will forever last.

You bring out the best in me whenever I need to
be at ease, or even chained from life's struggles;
just your presence brings me back to a place
where my soul finds peace and grace.

Hold My Hand

Take my hand so we can walk steadily through the
land, and take on any storm that comes our way,
because our love is continuously here to stay.

Can you be the candle in the dark for me,
so when everything around me goes dark
your hand I can take to lead me out?

Take my hand I ask, so we may fulfill our task to
love each other for the rest of our lives; from there
everything else on our love will certainly provide.

Hold my hand ever so tight and please never let go; just to
let you know, you're the one I feel deeply within no matter
what time of day. Your spirit within me is here to stay.

I Can't Settle

To settle for the things I truly don't
need would be a sin indeed.

I can't settle for less than what I deserve, because
my spirit will be restless and ever disturbed.

I know I need the true love in my life and someone who
will understand; while diligently taking my hand.

My son depends solely on me to find his happiness
and loving me will be to love him, so I must wait
upon that man to fulfill the divine plan.

At this stage of life, when I've experienced most
things, settling would be my demise and I refuse
to ever live a lie, because those shoes are very
uncomfortable and I can not remain to be subtle.

If settling is what I'm faced with now, then I choose to be
alone, for this girl can't give herself to another man. My
body was created for one man, and I will denounce the
master's plan if now I share my love with some other man.

My Oasis

Entering into a dimly lighted room, feeling the presence of
peace embracing me; I feel a fresh, clean spirit cradle me.

In my oasis is a reflection of my spirit and soul,
searching for the clean space of happiness forevermore.
While I sleep, a Buddha face I see, exuding the
tranquility of purity and love around me.

The energy is very strong while I transition into a different
land, not remembering all the things that went wrong.

My mind travels in my oasis, telling me to look deep
within, for this is where I will find myself one last time. I
surround myself with things that remind me of who I am;
needless to say my oasis is to please no man, but to let me
reminisce on the blessings that will enter once I remain in
my own midst, and show myself love from this day on.

Destiny Will Unveil

I believe in destiny and our love is the reason, because two
persons who can't stop loving from near or far; it doesn't
matter if we're apart. We still see love in each other's eyes.

Destiny is not something we reach out and touch, but in
time it will reveal and then from both of us love will never
hide, bringing us to the realization that was pushed aside.

Destiny is the mystery of tomorrow, but we must have
faith while we go through life's sorrows, knowing
that the rainbow will exude at the end when the
story is over and into fruition our love will mend.

So let us wait just a little bit longer, while destiny plays
its role and unveils the story that will never have an end,
because this love was truly cultivated by the master's
hand, so upon our hearts he will forever rest his hands.

I'm Ready

I'm ready to rest on your chest and tell
you I think you're simply the best.

I'm ready to commit in whatever way I can, because
being alone much longer couldn't be the master's plan.

I'm ready to look into your eyes and tell you my heart;
the story that will have to come to an end; for life is too
short and on no one else I've been able to depend.

I'm ready to take your hand throughout the
night, letting you welcome me into morn, where
I will see my rainbow after the dawn.

I'm ready to give you all of me; the parts that have
been kept hidden for so long, because no one else
has been worthy of this gift that can glisten, and
they certainly don't take the time to listen.

I'm ready to share your world, no longer to be kept on hold,
but able to tell the entire world of my feeling that I share
inside, because you have been the only love to be my guide.

May Your Heart Rest

May your heart rest assured knowing that my
love has not fallen overboard, but to you I respect,
even though at times it seems like neglect.

I give to you no overload, which only blows
the fuse of energy that is stored.

May you be at rest knowing this was a true test
that we both needed to pass, because once again
it comes to prove that love does last, even though
life gives us challenges and tedious tasks?

May your heart find a shelter that it can abide
and from vigor and strain continue to hide?

May your heart rest when you need to soothe your mind
and just the thought of me allows you to unwind?

So this message I send out to you, from near or far,
letting you know no matter where you are, our hearts
will rest in each other's arms as long as life goes on.

One Plant Of The Same Tree

One plant that grows from the same
tree is what defines you and me.

Our thoughts are intertwined like the root that veins
into each vine; your heart is beating each beat of mine.

We see from each other's eyes, making the
connection heavenly and divine.

Just like the leaf of a tree is how your
love penetrates life into me.

Each leaf receiving energy from the sun to grow and extend
the production plan to continue to decorate the land with
the blossom of new growth, allowing us to visualize our
future materialized in the cultivation of each other's eyes.

The Blindfolds Of Love

Every angle of the word *love* needs a cover that should
shield the heart, so you at times don't get torn apart.

The blindfolds of love sometimes can bring strength to
renew, but there are others that just turn you into fools.

The blindfold of love has many shapes and sizes, which
make you- linger on in, a world of no compromises.

Take the time to analyze and shortly thereafter
come to realize that the blindfolds are present
to make you oblivious to the signs of positive
reflections, which can beam into your eyes.

The Body And The Heart

The physical and the heart play two different
roles in this journey we take in life.

The body can find comfort at times, being
alone, or tolerate someone to full the emptiness
in the silence of a lonely mode.

The heart will ponder, if in someone's arms they don't
belong and the physical then finds ease, but the heart then
will be dis-eased. The heart is a vessel that reaches out
beyond the physical touch; it's eager to fulfill the desires of
the soul;, making you completely whole and rest assured,
while in its feeling you can then become conqueringly bold.

Many persons try to lie to the heart by lying
with persons wrong from the start, but then you
realize that only your physical gets pleasure for
a moment, and the heart is lingering beyond
measure to get fulfillment so you can treasure.

See, these two beings play two functions; let's not
confuse these emotions, but instead we should
place perspectives on our hearts; then one day
we will walk the journey to never be apart.

Too Busy

So many persons are too busy for each other,
but when the day should come that we are gone,
your heart suddenly longs to hear the whisper
of that voice that kept you warm inside.

Never be too busy for a friend, because at
times you don't know that a lifeline you could
have been, but you left them to sink.

We feed off of each other every day and when
a person is too busy to show you care, then
that leaves me to question the true affair.

You Can't Walk Away Then Return To Play

My emotions are not a merry-go-round for you to
take on a ride, hoping on whenever you feel free, then
leaving me to take the journey on wonderland spree.

You can't take me for granted when your heart is in need,
but when your life seems free you suddenly seek me.

You can't be too busy to return a call, because
that only tells me I'm not in your mind at all.

You can't demonstrate these things, and
don't expect me to hesitate and think.

Don't come my way to show me love one day,
and then from me you're gone to stay.

Above The Clouds

Above the clouds is where our love can float, as
long as we don't hesitate and linger about.

Let the love set its flight up high, and soar like
the doves in the sky. They fly over us each day,
letting us know our love is here to stay.

We can meet the stars for once and sweep them
in our hands to give us the vibrant feeling that
love is splendor, just waiting for us to capture.

One-Way Ticket

There is a one-way ticket with my
name this I know is the game.

When I take this journey, which leads to happiness, I
can't return on a flight, because a one-way passenger
I will be, never again to see confusion or fury.

On this flight the pilot calls out my name, making
me move to the cockpit for a while to watch the
clouds throughout the sky. Each cloud called out my
name telling me there is no end to the journey I will
take, because the clouds are there to cushion the falls
that I had throughout, but conquered them all.

I never wanted to take a one-way flight so
badly, but this one was destined for me, so
all the richness in life I would see.

The destination of this flight was called eternal
happiness, a place where not many have gone,
but I waited for my turn, so on this flight I now
board, never to know sadness no more

Friday Night

Friday night, you left a text but your message I didn't get; I hope you didn't receive a feeling of neglect.

Isn't it ironic how you dream to me that same night, not knowing you was reaching out to me?

I'm sorry I missed your message; I hope you're feeling alright, because your face I would have loved to see.

Do you need me to talk and confide your fear, or help you compartmentalize all your compromises.

What ever you might feel on this Friday night, know one thing, I was by your side; even if my face you didn't glimpse in your space.

Physical Pain

Why do I feel the physical pain of your emotional strain?

My body takes on all your feelings, which causes me
ache until I kneel down to pray on behalf of your sake.

The physical pain was not released until I got down on
my knees. Then, I call out your name; asking God to take
on the battles, so from your soul will hide the hassle.

I experience all of what you feel, but in
physical pain it comes to me.

Does this tell me you're my assignment—to help
you through your time of confinement?

When You're Feeling Down

When you're feeling down and things appear
distant and no longer seem profound, remember
things will certainly come back around.

In the valley is where you will find your true sense
of purpose and clarity in a peace of mind helping
you take on the battles of life with a desired tackle
to keep focus remaining at its proper level.

Always take a long hard look into your soul, and remember
the peace in the valley will give you the grace to grow
old knowing you're destined to touch the lives of others
with your innocent perception of sharing your laughter.

When down in the valley, it can be a very
still place to be, but when you remain true
your soul will continuously be free.

Take the time that you're given to capture the love
inside, and share your beauty with others, who have
love hidden and from themselves they want to hide.

Dining By The Water

The water sends a secret message to me while I sit and
eat; telling me it feels my heart and knows how much
my heart lives amongst the freedom of its depth.

Sitting there feeding my body while the ocean
fed my mind, spirit, and soul; giving off the
night air to feel completely whole.

There is so much richness in the stillness of your presence
a value that money will never be able to measure. We
just need to appreciate and enjoy the moment forever.

Silence in the Stillness

There is such silence in the stillness of a moment,
allowing you to reflect upon all your imbedded power.

Only in the silence can we see all the things
that were meant to be. There are no distractions
in that moment; keeping your heart on a ride
that will only end up in deceit and lies.

While you're in the stillness of the hour just meditate on the
power that life can bring, once you surrender everything.

Can Time Return?

People are at play not taking time out of their busy
day to tell someone just how much they care.

Once time has departed from us, it will never return; like
the soul that has lost its way in life, hoping that some kind
person would extend a hand to help it along the way.

Time goes by slowly when in hope you live, but
never during this time should we forget to give.

Sometimes we are only given one opportunity to capture
the moment caused in that stillness of time, so let's do
whatever it takes not to waste a moment of time.

Mellow Moments

Sitting back inhaling the essence of the mellowness
of the moment, while clarity is in the air, my
mind is clear; from confusion my soul hides.

Looking deeply within for the tranquil peace
of mind that is hidden way down inside.

How many persons can say they have these
moments within a day? Or are they content with
the distractions that create a state of confinement,
which only leads to an emotional assignment?

Mellow moments are not a bad venue to visit,
once your soul needs quick renewal from
the repeated rituals of life's menu.

Always Leave The Cage Open

When your love goes away someday, just like
that pigeon that leaves to soar, always leave
the cage open for it to revert home.

Whenever you soar, your wings into the world then
you realize there was nothing left to learn; you will
enter in the open doorway left for you to return.

The door will have an open way at all times in my
heart, so if you find your way back to me, I will
shelter you from the world and all its tart.

This Love

This love that I give to you is the gift of a treasure
from above, and in this lifetime never will you
find another love so true. So baby, listen to
the message of my love sent out to you.

This love is not condescending, leaving behind
the pretentious functions of this world, only
giving my love to you so profound.

Will you take my love, I ask? Let us both fulfill our
hearts' desire, because this love will never expire.

Does Having My Heart Make You Feel Good?

There is no more damage that one heart can endure,
but do you feel secure knowing you have my heart?

You can take my heart and shatter it once more,
but from pain I have made it secure.

A woman can always show a man her strength
if she desires, but sometimes we need to hold on
to faith while displaying enormous grace.

If having my heart only makes you feel like a man,
then on that promise you can continue to stand.

Gentle Kisses

Gentle kisses that you gave through the years;
never once did you bring these eyes to tears.

I want back these gentle kisses in my life, even if from
another they will have to come, because when I remember
the gentleness my heart transforms to life again keeping
the feeling alive to have love spring into my life.

Bring back the gentle kisses again; the sweetest
kiss that makes my body tremble at the
thought of your gentle kiss upon my lips.

Reservations For Two

This evening I made reservations for two. Can
I ask of you simply not to reschedule?

This reservation we both need to keep so the
transition our souls can seek never again allowing
our hearts to be lonely or unpleasantly bleak.

The table has our names delicately placed,
so our seating will have no mistakes.

Your heart will feel each beat of mine; while we
celebrate the evening over a glass of wine.

When the reserved evening for two has come to an end;
love will restore our hearts once again and enhance
the vibrancy to each other to absolutely no end.

Each Step I Take

Each step I take, I secretly reflect on the journey that I
traveled, embracing life and challenging all its battles.

Each step had a different triumph, leaving
me at times completely solemn.

While I strive to the next step above all the rest, I keep the
momentum in my path so the step will be shortened at last.

When I arrive at the last step to enter the doorway
of eternal peace, I will unveil the virtuous vision
and reflect once again on my mission.

Healing

Healing flies on the wings of mercy, and it pitches
on the pavement of love and forgiveness.

Healing mends the heart of pain while one is
struggling through emotional bondage and strain.

Wrap yourself in the bandage of bliss, so the
repair process your emotions won't miss.

Let us extend a helping hand toward the healing
process making one another the product of success.

Power Of Agreement

How do I walk with you if your vision I
can't see? The pathway is dark and no light
of agreement shines down on me.

In order to walk in unity; the power of
agreement needs to be free so we can take the
stroll toward union and our destiny.

See, the power of agreement is where I need to abide,
so that union can continue to reside right by my side.

Your Love Has A Hold On Me

The love that you give has such a hold on me that has an
end less story untold.

Your love cradles me in the depth of sorrow; your
hand only in that time I need to borrow.

Your love has been the tranquilizer for my
mind, released like one capsule at a time.

Only you have had such a hold on me through the years,
never using harsh words to bring these eyes to tears.

Eighteen Years Old

To be eighteen is a tender age; to have love
capture your heart and place it in a cage.

I was eighteen when into your eyes I looked; then
became helplessly hooked. I was swallowed by your soul,
leaving me yearning for you even when I became old.

How I would do whatever it takes to rewind life from all the
mistakes, and fast forward to a chapter where love resides,
because we both have longed for laughter in our lives.

We were both eighteen then. Our age was
only separated by three months apart, but that
tender age brought true love to our hearts.

Above and Beyond

Love goes above and beyond the usual call.

Over the hilltop, climbing the highest mountain peak;
to see the one you love full of laughter and so meek.

Obstacles can never stop love, because the emotions
come with force that binds the chains that hinder
the everlasting kindred that are yours and mine.

Above and beyond is the destination our love
should reach, so we can share the ecstasy of love
and glance at the negativity true love can defeat

Empathy

Empathy is not something many persons have, but
when you experience the trials of life, your heart can
sympathize with emotions from others that come about.

Why is it, some persons need to experience
that walk to be able to show grace to that man,
who no longer has a smile on his face?

If you only do unto others as you'd like it done unto you,
there would be no need to face some of life's abuse.

Let us show empathy to each person we meet,
regardless if you haven't walked in their feet.

Time To Move On

The time has come for my heart to find a place,
where it can start to find the love I need.

This is the only place that peace resides and
success will be in the doorway of my life.

Time is something that waits on no man, because
only time truly knows the relevant plan.

To move forward is not an awkward place to be; instead
I reflect on all the good memories and keep them from
all harm, but it's now time for my heart to move on.

Last Chance

Chances come only once in a lifetime. To
live in regret is torture on one's mind.

Did you do everything possible in your world to
keep the memory of our love alive, or did you stifle it
with your continuous strife you have in your life?

I never want to live my life with regrets, but
a chance for love, I won't neglect.

Don't ask my heart to answer anymore questions you may
have, because I truly gave you love for the last chance.

I Will

I will find true love someday, even if
from me it seems so far away.

I will find someone to take my hand, and
from danger secure my soul so I will one
day share with them and grow old.

I will love the way I was taught; never to
bring fear into someone else's heart.

I will rest all cares on your shoulder, for you to
give me the lift I need to become stronger.

When I'm weak; I'll extend my hand, and I
know you will be there for me to stand.

I will love you for the rest of my life, because
that is the true definition of a wife.

Black Bird

Black bird, does your sky look gray on this cloudy
summer day, or are you just simply enjoying the play
while you perch on the tree, looking down at me?

Wherever you go, you are always free to fly
about. No confinement does your wings
wear, flying throughout the air.

You chirp occasionally with a sigh of relief that so
many persons can only preach, and when you're tired
to soar, you then rest your wings on a tree branch while
your soul takes a rest from the evolutional launch.

Will Our Paths Cross Again?

Should our paths take the turn that winds up on
the avenue of each other's hearts, or will we repeat
the historical cycle that has kept us apart?

Will our path intertwine again one day and
remain in the pathway of love to stay?

Our hearts suffer each second that they beat; not being
able to share the love and shower the harmony to our feet.

If ever our paths decide to cross again, let us not allow
it to take a detour bend that delays love to blossom,
and a return-to sender message then we will send.

From This Day On

From this day on is what you said when you held me
in your arms, promising to let no one come before.

This promise I didn't believe. I felt in time we will
eventually see. If this will materialize, then once
again I can confide and pray you will shield me from
all harm, while you rock me gently in your arms.

From this second day of June; our journey with each other
can only bloom, so on your promise I will stand; sheltering
my heart and extending to our love a vibrant new start.

Navy Lodge

While I patiently sat waiting to be checked in, my
mind could do nothing but recollect the memories
of you, so that left me soundlessly subdued.

Was this where my love was based?
Memories kept reflecting your face.

I felt your presence over me ever so strong, but
I never knew this was your base, but once again
destiny lead me back into your space.

The Navy took away my true love, and since then my life
hasn't been the same, but my heart has always remained.

A Ton Of Bricks

Conducting your business in a diurnal way, you said the
thought of me suddenly hit you in a brick-like way.

Suddenly the beam shined in your eyes, making
you now realize the person who cares for you the
most was being treated like a ghost—someone
who might appear, but truly wasn't there.

When it hit like a ton of bricks in the afternoon,
I think those thoughts didn't come too soon,
but now that you're enlightened, I hope our
relationship will be enormously brightened.

The Smiles Come So Naturally

Your smiles come so naturally whenever you're with me.

This is the person I love to see, when you smile and gallivant so playfully. For a moment your cares are wiped away and on the present experience your heart will stay.

One after the other is what I see, when they're coming back at me. Telling the tale of your heart and your emotions are then worn on the sleeve of beatitude; exploring the real person beneath the muzzle of life's hustle and bustle.

The Valley

In the valley is somewhere no one wants to be, but
this lonely place was a learning experience for me.

When you're in the valley, the mountains seems so oversized
and no longer do you have the faith to survive, but the
day will arrive for your experience again to come alive.

Just take this time to reacquaint with one self,
because this is a learning process, you see, and
clarity the valley will eventually reveal.

When the doors open again, then you can remember
the moment in the valley and be thankful to
be able to enter the doorway of elevation that
will have you no longer in isolation.

Power Of Freedom

Power derives from activity, which needs to be free.

Freedom is the unrestraint of vocal liberty, which
longs to accommodate in power continually.

To be free to be one self in situations that
might restrain your power and your soul is the
place that each individual wishes to be.

Evolve your power to the next dimension, where
freedom can be spoken without retention and easily
acted upon, leaving no space for any exemptions.

Driving Down Memory Lane

When I drove down memory lane, I looked to my right and there I would see the reflecting thoughts of you and me. When I looked to my left; I was kept reminiscing on the places that we visited, letting me ride on; there I came to the intersection where we both met, taking me back down love's lane. I decided to take the right turn, but only then you made the left, which kept us from each other for oh so long. How do we find our way to each other on these lonely roads? No streetlights do I see while trying to find my way. I will pull up to the stop sign down on memory lane, and wait there until I can go on. It's easier if I wait right here until you find me again, because everywhere I go from here no one will have all of my heart, and I always fall apart.

Fulfilling Your Own Dream

Dreams are like butterflies waiting for somewhere to land.

Holding on to your own dream is the only hope
to fulfill your master's plan for your life.

Keep the faith strong and there will always
be someone telling you to hold on.

Materializing your dream is the ultimate start in allowing
peace and tranquility to come into your heart.

Love Heals All Wounds

Contrary to popular belief; many think time heals all
wounds, but instead I would to them say love is the healer
of all wounds, bringing you back from emotional abuse.

Taking the time to show love is certainly the
way to compromise and make it stay.

Emotional scars take longer to heal than those, which
were imparted on your physical by someone.

Healing your wounds does take time, but when
love is shown you will be more than fine.

Memories

Memories are the reflections of the
cornerstones of our minds.

Sometimes we experience pleasant or negative
milestones. While reflecting we recapture the pleasant
ones deposited upon our lives. When we reflect on
the dismay some negative input may have caused,
but yet to affirm our strength in years to come.

Embrace your memories, perpetually keeping those close
to your thoughts, which will then escort you to your divine
purpose someday, and continually warm your heart!

Mirror

Mirror, mirror on my wall, you seem to be the fairest one
of them all; seeing many people look in, trying to capture
a completeness that sometimes is in their meekness.

If only you could speak to reflect the many
things you've seen through persons seeming to be
perfect, but in their lives they live with regret.

You reflect to each person themselves, coming
to you as who they are they are, but some can't
stand to stare, because you show them what is
fare Then everything becomes crystal clear.

Mirror, mirror will still stand tall to tell the story behind
the walls to people who sometimes can't take a fall.

You speak clearly what you see: a soul reflecting back
sometimes. Many are in such lack of being their true
selves; hiding behind the camouflage of pretence.

Never Let Me Lose You

Your love is like the ocean breeze that eases my
heart at the moment to make the feeling cease
Your strength has been my anchor when the ships
sail by, leaving me to wonder if this journey was
meant to be for me alone to sail the seas.

I lose most things in life that my heart is fond of, but
without your friendship again I will be left to ponder.

Thanks for all the moments that we've shared,
and in love's atmosphere these memories will stay,
keeping me fresh when the skies seems so gray.

I thought I lost your friendship once in the past, and there
was no feeling of splendor that arrived that would last.

Don't ever take away your hand from me to extend; when
from this world I just want to hide, because even though
you don't know it; those hands have always been my guide.

Relevant Authority

They say changes come about from an initial dream; most recognized persons took the leap with faith from dream to reality, becoming relevant authority contributors, making changes to an era of life, whether present of future.

Poets have the authority; oh how much I hope they see. The world can appreciate the word of a poet materialized from a thought or even a dream, and on paper many have made the relevant authority real.

My definition of a relevant authority is a man of value respected by many, who will demonstrate a structured pattern in his own life before displaying authority to those of a place, making decisions so unique to elevate.

Wedding Day

The wedding day when everyone came out to play;
celebrating two hearts that will beat as one, watching
while the bride and groom take each other's hands.

Into the depth of love they will now abide, leaving
behind the phenomenon world of false pride,
being able to express their love from this day on,
and waiting to hold each other for a lifespan!

Window Treatment

Window treatment, how you cover all the faults that are
within; making it so easy to appear happy and bright and
leaving no evidence of spectators throughout the night.

You shut out the world with your beauty,
reflecting peace and tranquility.

Oh window treatment, if only we could comprehend
the things you have to cover up from within;
sometimes I know it's painful for you to see.

It's a good thing that you're temporarily fixed, so no
emotions do you show while you hang in someone's abode.

Young Love

Two young hearts is what we were, waiting for the world
to take us in and capture our hearts in a love spin.

Imbedded were our spirits, minds, and souls no
matter where we both were. I feeling you and you
feeling me is exactly why we were meant to be!

Are you the other half of me? I ask. Just like twins
born together, feeling the pain of the other is what
we are. How does the universe explain this to me?

Even when our hearts grew older; our love
for each other only grew stronger. So to you,
my love, I will say: Just like the deep blue sea,
please keep the faith hidden deeply for me.

A WOMAN IN LOVE

A woman in love will do most anything to capture that
man within.
A woman in love doesn't see things that will cause her
pain, because she's only looking for future gain.
A woman in love sometimes have no fear; diving into
love without a life vest to protect her heart to sail back
to shore, where she can immediately get rest.
A woman sees no wrong in a man that has placed her
on a love spell bound for oh so long.
A woman seeks love and affection each day, but at
times her love will be dismayed; causing a rejection in
her life.
To this woman I would say, continue your faith in love
comes what may!

LAUGHTER

The feeling that is imbedded within comes now from inside to brighten your world and give you pride.

The ray of sunshine will flow on your face; allowing it to be a natural phase.

Persons looking on can only see a pleasant demeanor each time, which makes them wonder in their minds how someone who still has strife can where a smile throughout their life.

Reality

Living in a world where most things appear
false, how can reality even last?

Real characteristics are buried within, so from
condescending your heart will spring.

Keep it real, to all I say, never allowing
pretentious characteristics to take a prey
on your life throughout the day.

BROKEN HEARTED CLOWN

A clown has many faces, but when the
heart of a happy demeanor
has been broken the face of a clown
no longer has the radiance.

Look into the eyes I say; the face is
made of disguise, but the
eyes invite the world into its brokenness,
and blue state of mind.

Look at all the clowns in the world I
ask. What makes this one
so different is the far away teardrop
in the eyes and the piercing
feeling left from a broken heart.

Can this clown be mended again I
ask? As I look on and feel
all the aftermath. Pick yourself up I
would say, brush yourself
off get ready to face another day.
Look at all the other clowns
around you and notice the only
difference is the feeling from
yourself you don't hide; while every
other clown continues to live
a lie!

Phenomenal Woman

I am a phenomenal woman, but being such
a woman comes with a high price!

Everyone always seems to describe me as such a strong
woman, which are very high standards to live by.

In a world filled with people, you would
often think you are not alone; however, you
find yourself lost and no one is there.

How sheltered I now feel from everyone; all that I
have loved is all gone now. Why? I often find myself
seeking for answers, some of which I may never find.

Why after all the battles that have been conquered,
I then feel I lost it all? I wonder why?

CHINA CABINET

China cabinet there you stand tall with your back against
the wall, and in behind your doors I see the entire world's
finest crockery.

When I look at you I see elegance encountering the breeze,
while you wait for someone to share their special moments
with you.

Only once in a lifetime you come out to play; then cleaned
and polished your put away. Just like some persons whose
heart now hides; you share your beauty with only those that
are deserving of. To them your love will never be denied.

CHINA CABINET

COMING IN AND OUT OF YOUR LIFE

Years have elapsed since we saw each other last, but why
does the Universe keep taking us back in each others arms?

Coincidences in life don't happen this often; everything
that takes place is God's way of showing his face,
existence, and his grace. Giving us the opportunity to take
the leap, and one day we will be at each others feet.

You're the best thing that ever happened to me then; silly
of me for my youth, but I know I've always told you the
truth; leaving the decision entirely up to you, not creating
any confusion in your mind, but allowing you to get the
peace you needed to find!

ENCOURAGING WORDS

Encouraging words is what you've always
shared with me; even when I
didn't have them to return.

What you saw for my life through your
own spirit being your guide you
would share with me so I could see the light.

Feelings for each other are a real quality
that not everyone possesses
unless to yourself you are true, and to
the other honesty from them you
should never hide. It is up to the person
whether they accept or deny.

How could I thank you for sharing your
encouraging thoughts with me
holding me up when I was down, bringing
me back into my safe zone.

Never stop encouraging and sharing
your light that God so diligently
blessed you with the pearl like eyes

You I will also never forget, and my soul
says thanks for bringing out
the pains, and soothing me back to accomplish all the gains.

EVERYTIME I LOOK AT YOU

There is always something new to discover when I
look into your eyes.

The feeling of pride is portrayed in each
look; making me feel divinely hooked.

Your eyes have a mysterious distance to them and
whenever I look I'm drawn into your soul; leaving
my countenance endlessly whole.

GIRLS NIGHT OUT

Down came the night; busy street lights
flashing, people crossing while we watched on
ready to escape the world for a night.
All the girls laughing, and reminiscing on the
past; remembering what it was like when love
use to last.
There we were having a few drinks; listening
and waiting to be approached by some
gentleman giving a line, but we all laughed and
told them it's our time.
Isn't it nice to have a night where we can be
our true selves; letting our hair down and
acting like clowns.
We must be willing to share with each other
when the load is too much for you to bear. Oh
girls we must do this again; relaxing and truly
being friends. Wanting to capture all the
joy from life and willing to bend so that
situations will definitely mend.

HAMMOCK BY THE SEA

Let us swing into eternity, where everyone is free
and here by the sea we can feel the ocean breeze.

Plunge into the hammock with me; letting us both
relax and be at ease to encounter love fall at our ease,
and then we can seize the moment to capture the
natural breeze while swinging under the tree.

HURT

H- Harboring ill feelings towards someone who has done you wrong, but hoping to let these feelings go when you heal.

U- Unusual emotions that shuffle through your mind, but being mature enough to realize.

R- Ruling your emotion during such time isn't easy, but with rest you will be fine.

T- Trusting again in the power of Love is extremely hard. Keep the faith and learn to be patient, then trust will exude itself in time.

We have all shared this emotion one time or another, but let us learn never to allow it to hither us from our purpose of sharing as we go; making the best of our emotions later on down the road!

I DID IT MY WAY

I hold my head up high as I go, because I know I did things my way; leaving me with few regrets, and I certainly couldn't ask for less.

In my heart the feelings lied, and to my mind I couldn't deny. I was never brought up to lie, and play games with people's minds. This is why I couldn't give you all of me, instead I allowed destiny to play its role achieving my goal.

I have no regrets for this you see, because truly this was meant to be, and time is certainly the key element in conquering me.

God knows the reason for all things, so in him I place by faith; allowing him to hold my hands through the storms and guiding me through the night; making conscious decisions that is right for my life.

Escaping The World

The world at times is a lonely place to be, even
though amongst each other we seem so free.

Every moment you get a chance, remember to seek for the
bigger plan; not depending on anyone to extend a helping
hand. This at times to achieve, you must escape your
present situation and begin the process of self-evaluation.

The world is noisy and hectic for me, so
whenever I seek freedom for a while, I capture
the escape of the world in my mind.

This condition is truly not the norm, but instead to
survive, I escape from the world and all its lies.

People don't understand this procedure,
because it takes away from the world and its
rituals, leaving you totally miserable.

I NEED YOU

Needing someone everyday and night is a blessing in Disguise, and to our heart be no demise. Let's just look deeply into each other eyes.

You were made for me and me for you. Just like the left foot was made for the right; I need you always by my side.

You bring the fresh breeze in the summer time that calms me which state of mind I'm in and always bring me back to life again.

A need is different from a want. Those that run after have intentions my dear, but I've let you soar standing by the side never to mention how deeply I feel; watching you grow into your person fill of character and grace each time I look into your face.

LET ME BE YOUR FREEDOM

If I were your freedom it would be not for just one
season, but for a lifetime we would share and seldom
would we not care to express the heart's desire to be
free.

Let me loosen the chains that bind your feet,
so together we can live in sweet harmony.

Let me be your freedom even for just one season; to
give your heart the reason to mellow out in the
freedom of tranquility.

Let me off the Roller Coaster

Up and down we go again;
playing life's longest roller
coaster ride, but whenever we
look in each others eyes we
know this is where we belong
singing each other's happy song.

The crowd looks on while we
play; waiting for that final day
when we no longer make the
barriers of life get in the way,
and to the world be true; even if
it cause a brew.

No matter how often we ride; it
feels like the first; waiting to
hold each other through it all,
and keeping our heads up above
the storm

LOVE AT FIRST SIGHT

How can two people love at first sight? To
each other the feeling was so right; leaving
an earth's shimmer just like dynamite.

There we were for the pristine time interlocking
our eyes, and afterwards then came our minds.

A phone call I wanted to make to you
after our meeting, shy about
it; I still persisted. Then to get the
shock of my life realizing the
phone line would not ring, because
there you were doing the very
same thing. Why doesn't the phone
ring I uttered into the phone.
Hello I said, and who is this. Leaving me mesmerized and
surprised; suddenly you replied with your name.

Ever since, I've asked myself why did this
experience even exist? Why can't we over twenty
two years let each other go? Will this
question ever be answered?

Dear Lord, tell me why this man came into my life
and wrapped his arms around me for my entire life?

Why Do I Feel Love Is A Lie?

Tonight I believe that love is a lie, and this
feeling I will certainly not deny.

All my life, I've shared feeling so deep, but
these feelings life shattered back to sleep.

My heart is still, but feels to move on and I no
longer want to have faith in anything or anyone.

Why is love such a lie? People try to convince themselves
that they are happy, but true love they continue to refuse.

Why do you create this world to feel these emotions,
when only thing it causes is true commotion?

I want to be alone from this day on;
never to give my heart to anyone.

LOVE HAS NO PRICE TAG

Love can't be found in a department
store tagged with a price or
value.

Love is the least expensive thing to
share, but yet the most costly
to gain!

Love is the one thing in life that has no value, but the most
expensive and most rare commodity to acquire.

Love is yet so free in all abundance
and caring in its personality.
Although it doesn't possess a price
tag and many people pass it
by preferring to purchase things of
no longevity for their lives.

I will continue to let the rays of
freeness pour into my spirit by
accepting all the gifts it has to offer from up above.

Thank you Lord for not attaching a
price to this precious gift
that flows so freely, and blessing me
with so much of your Love!

The Girls With The Frills

The girls with the frills get everything. Don't
men see the heart behind a face and know
that with time the frills will erase?

Girls, who want the fancy things—exercising
only material things—get everything.

Girls that are real at heart, men take for granted and
tear apart; not seeing the inner beauty of that heart.

Why not only want material gain; maybe
this would cause so much less pain.

I need to be a girl of just frills and no longer use my
personal skills, because the road to happiness is so very
false and no man truly appreciates my humble cause.

LOVE IS LIKE BUILDING A HOUSE

When a house is first constructed; the foundation is formed; thereafter the structure is created, and when the stability is there the final step comes in by placing the covering.

Well, Love is the very same thing. First you meet someone; secondly the foundation is formed, which is trust. If trust is treated with Respect then the second level of elevation will take place.

Next you have the sharing, and caring process for each other, which is the covering and shield for the Love you have found.

Once the trust is no longer the ingredient; your foundation of Love will come stumbling down. Without trust caring and sharing will also eliminate; making Love no longer a pleasure, but now a big mistake.

NO ONE COULD TAKE YOUR PLACE

For years I've tried, but to myself only I lied; trying to replace a diamond with pebbles that had no shine.

Your love from me you took away, and in my heart you were there to stay. I didn't know that you were to depart and from me be gone. I felt so alone only to share my love with someone else who never valued me like a gem.

We were young, but even so in my heart I've always kept your song holding me together when everything around me went wrong.

No one could take your place throughout life. I've tried for oh so long.

My love to you I must surrender, and throw my heart on the line letting you know before I depart; giving you always that special part of my heart.

PEARL-THE REAREST GEM

The pearl is found in the sea; the most rear thing to me, so
when you find yourself such a gem; like a rose on a stem
you must treat with gentle kindness oh so meek.

Like the warmth of the meadow you should treat your pearl
without a shadow of doubt, knowing that the gift you found
will bring you love so profound.

White in color just like the purity that lies within; you see
the splendor created by the oyster, which makes your heart
then lust after to capture the beauty thereafter.

To a pearl I would say; let your beauty always stay rear and
mysterious to mankind, because its in your rearness
you will find the greatest peace of mind.

SPEED YOUR LOVE TO ME

This is where you belong; once you said to me, but never did I reply, because through your eyes I needed you to realize that here is where you should be.

Destiny can never tear us apart; from the start we have captured each others heart. Mistakes we both made in our lives, and ask me if you need to know in regards to living a lie.

Speed your love to me I would ask, so we both can continue the task that will face us each day, but in the evenings we shall play; to capture all the bliss that we have missed, doing it with our kiss.

Tell Me

Tell me you care not just for a moment's pleasure,
but also for conditions without measure.

Tell me the most intimate desires of your heart, so that
one-day we might build on them and never be apart.

Tell me when you're afraid, so I can be the shelter
of security for just that season even if your heart
doesn't give you a good enough reason.

Tell me what you might feel I can correct in
myself to make our relationship better, as long as
you don't want to alter this person forever.

Tell me when you're hurting, so I can help
ease your pain, even though with the bond
we share there is so much more to gain.

Tell me all of your felicity, so we can elevate our
relationship to the next level of prosperity.

The Attentiveness In Your Touch!

Your touch exudes much Love and gentleness!

Your smile is similar to having an encounter
with your own amusement park capturing
all the blissful, joyful wonders from
within.

Your kiss is a security blanket that shelters the heart
from the stormy weathers, and whenever I am in your
presence there is such a peaceful countenance that
illuminates; allowing the entire atmosphere to scintillate.

Just like the existence of the Universe, you are one of
the reasons why the sun rises in the mornings, and the
moon and the stars fabricate their appearance at night!

Thank You For Being The Person Who You Are !

The Gift Of Loving Yourself!

The key element to the art of Loving
Yourself is to know, and truly
understand you. In order to do so, at
times one should withdraw from
their surroundings, which provides you
with that time needed to listen to
the inner spirit speak.

After familiarizing with yourself and being able to
evaluate you; can you then truly look yourself in
a mirror and say the words "Yes I Love You"?

Only after perfecting the art of Loving Yourself
can you then truly express Love to the magnitude
in which it should be expressed to
others!

THERE WE GO AGAIN

When you speak I would love to believe, but
my heart is on hold always waiting for the
story to unfold.

Words mean a lot to me now. Many talk and
oh how it's cheap; like evaporation with the
breeze.

I want to know that your words are true,
and disappointment with you will be few.

How can I take this leap to love again; yes
in you I did find my very best friend, but
love is too deep to once again take a fall that
is very steep.

Self-Inflicted Pain

Some pain is self-inflicted, just like the wound
that remains open to constantly receive rigor.

Why do persons try to capture the heart of someone;
when they know it belongs to another?

When you demonstrate this act; you're only causing your
whole world to lack, because the same one that you've
entrapped will never treat you any better than just that.

You might turn around and say this wasn't
supposed to be this way, but before you
accuse, please take a long look at you!

Entrapment can only produce one act, just like the
animal that is caged unwillingly and desires to be set
free. This is the meaning of entrapment to me.

These results in self-inflicted pain, causing
both parties involved not ever to gain.

Climb Any Mountain

I need a love that will climb any mountain and cross
any sea, just to prove his love is there with me.

I need a love that is not afraid to show emotions,
because this is when I'll see your heart's devotions.

Over any mountain and across any sea will your love come
for me? If the answer to this question is yes, my dear,
then in your hands I will place my heart for you to steer.

The mountains appear tall and the seas seem wide, but
if your love is everlasting it will certainly ride the tide.

Two Ships Sailing In The Night!

There we were our hearts adjoining for the pristine time.

In conversations your spirit feeling mine. Me feeling you. Suddenly in the stillness of the moment we ask ourselves why Our paths may have crossed in this lifetime?? Never the less, There is a little phrase that goes like this everything in life Happens for a wise purpose, a reason, and also for a season.

It is left entirely up to us to see the purpose; understand the Reason, and endure the season that our hearts adjoin like two Ships adjacent sailing in the night!

Unconditional Love

Love me without measure, and in return
there will be GREAT pleasure.
Love me in all of my pain, and thereafter
the magnitude of love will bring
forth GAIN.
Love me in sickness: even in my weakness.
Let me glimpse into your eyes
where there I will see the depth of my WEAKNESS.
Love me following the minimal levity of
weight gain, subsequently derived
from the arrival of our LOVE CHILD.
See Unconditional Love is really all I yearn
for; once accomplished we can
learn to savor the epicure of True Unconditional Love.

Walking In The Rain

Walking in the rain with one who means the
most to me, simply walking and kicking
back the breeze.

Walking in the rain hand in hand with my son,
the one true reason why I am who I am. See my
son in the only reason I take on my daily task to
see him grow and fulfill his purpose at last.

Whenever you can you should try walking in the rain with
someone dear by your side to see the laughter on their face
as the raindrops fall, and then nothing else in this world
for just a moment really matters!

WE HELD IT TOGETHER

We held our feeling for each other for so long; leaving an
impression on love for a lifespan.

How can two people love each other
for so long? Unconditionally
is how we held our love together. Both
watching each other from a
distance materializing information
of relationships in our lives;
leaving each other the space to perform and captivate all the
fantasies in our hearts always wondering
back in each other's arms.

I hope for love we hold it together a
while longer, because I know
now my heart cannot wonder. So I
leave the universe to take care
of our feelings and bring us back as long as we are willing.

My Personal Flight

While I took my personal flight, I had so
much desire that everything would be all right,
and I held on to hope ever so tight.

This flight means clarity for me, looking out
to the clouds, while they speak out so loud,
telling me that there is a turning point in my
life, which certainly won't cause me fright.

I take this flight alone today, leaving behind the
sadness and the gray that only makes my world dim,
causing me all these years never to see anything.

When I reach my destination, I will bring my
happiness to fruition and remember even if I stand
alone, I will not allow my heart to turn to stone.

The Act of Kindness

The Kindling spirit that in vehicles someone
to bestow generosity amongst others.

Acting on Kindness is a rear commodity in
today's society, but when you have the heart
of glare this act becomes a daily ritual
In the lives of others. One kind act portrayed in a
moment embraces Humanity for a Lifetime!

WEALTH

W-Weakness surrendered to monetary
funds and not mankind.

E- Eagerness some portray to accomplish
and rise above the other.

A-Agony experienced when the thought
of monetary agitation occurs.

L- Longing feel for love that can be obtained,
but doesn't possess a price tag.

T-Tasteless characteristics that derive once obtained.

H-Humility in everything is the vehicle to success.

Most persons take wealth as a sedative. The more
steps they climb on the ladder of success throughout
life; then the last step of humility gets left behind.
Wealth was not created just to give comfort, but
sanction one to having options. Once you obtain
wealth take the time to know you who are as a person
and don't surrender to the funds; allow the funds to
surrender to you!

WHAT IS POETRY?

Poetry is freedom to speak on paper.

Poetry is Love, and the ability to express your
most intimate emotions imbedded within.

Poetry is wisdom, because only a wise deep
individual can be in touch with the sensitive
side of themselves, and allow it to exude
itself in their lives.

Poetry is inspiration; giving everyone
that could possibly have the
opportunity of reading a script, and
then the changes thereafter of
making a lasting impression upon even one
individual with the remote possibility of bringing
forth a change in someone's lifestyle.

Last but certainly not least, poetry is
music, and as we all know
this is the main ingredient used to
reach the hearts of many. No
matter how different and unique we
all are, everyone relates to the
language of lyrics and rhythm.

Rise And Fall To Expectations

Stand up tall and challenge the rise
to the expectations of us all.
Do you conquer your defeat with the
expectations that lay at your feet?
Stand up tall and rise to each call so your
conquering battles will be remembered by all.
To rise above daily expectations is not simple
at all, but believe in yourself and the battles
will eventually become very small.

Harnessing Family Values

Let us harness family values again, so that
life will continue to hand you a friend.

Take a teaspoon of patience, adding a pinch
of sweetness to the glass, and finally stirring
in hope to complete the harness at last.

Each value will be imprinted daily throughout a
family that takes the time to map out principles.

Values derive from investing hard work, but moreover
they allow you the avenue to be free while the
family can discuss things in peace and harmony.

A House Is Not A Home

A house is not a home when we are so far apart; nor can
it be a home when no longer do I have your heart.

Together we made a family, sharing our goals and
inspirations, cultivating them into your children. A
role model for our offspring's to follow. But where
has this gone? To me there is no tomorrow.

Silly of you; can't you see no one will ever love
you the way I have—like the deep blue sea.

A chair is certainly not a chair to me when no one
ever sits there. Now that you're gone I no longer
have a home; to me it's now a house—existing,
taking up the necessary space with its size.

Come back to me, I ask. Remember the things that we
shared, and with another woman never will it last. The
things that other people tell you won't always be true, or
just for a moment's pleasure they come to you like wolves.

Our house is not a home without your smile keeping
me warm inside, and telling each other goodnight!

A Thought For The Day

Every woman has something in her past
that she would like to forget.

When things occur in our lives that hurt us deeply,
we learn to live with it as we would a migraine
headache, arthritis, or cramps. The symptoms
are different; nevertheless, it's all pain.

When we are hurting emotionally, we tell ourselves
that if we forget about it, it'll go away. Instead we keep
it in our subconscious; thus, the pain remains.

Always remember this simple lesson:

Forgetting is not a memory lapse; it is actually
a memory release. When you forget, you release
your pain and hurt, allowing your spirit to
elevate to a new level. It's called healing!!

Butterfly

Butterfly, butterfly takes me far away to a place
where one day there absolutely will be no gray.

Butterfly, can you see over yonder where my
soul yearns and ponders of the somber in the
enchantment disguised on the other side?

Let me be your wings for only one day; giving
me the reason to spring into the seasons, and
when I am weary upon a flower I will rest.
Butterfly, butterfly, your world is the best.

Humility

H- Humbling to the hearts of others. Hostility
is not a characteristic to obtain when humility
has entered the doorway of the heart.

U- Unassuming personality is one that
portrays itself under this umbrella.

M- Majestic feelings take over when
you possess this quality.

I- Involuntary loving action that suddenly portrays itself.

L- Love and loyalty will be a lucrative
combination thereafter.

I- Injecting humane characteristics into society.

T- Tutoring the nature of kindness amongst others
and taking the time to listen keenly to others speak.

Y- Yielding to selfish qualities; yearning the need to share,
love, and give of yourself to others whenever necessary.

Humility is a characteristic which in your youthful years
one usually don't possess, but like fine wine, the more
you age the finer you become in quality and demeanor.

It's All About You

It's all about you, simply. Can't you see?
Not once has it ever been about me.

Have you ever considered my emotions when you
vent your feelings inside, or perhaps as long as
you're happy and from pain you can hide?

There are times you speak, expecting no reply, but as long
as we share a relationship then may I ask, who am I? I
believe that we are a pair, and clearly that defines two.
Voicing my opinions, and not only keenly lending you my
ear... See? It's been all about you over these years, my dear.

Let's Go Sailing

Let us unfold the rapture of the seas; together
we can sail on the everlasting breeze.

Let us hold each other's hands ever so tight, and together we
will see that nature has too much to teach once we beseech.

Let us go sailing once again, I repeat, so we can eternally
allow the natural flow of water to come to our feet. While
we endeavor to have this treat, never must we forget the
pleasure to allure the intimacy of just simply going sailing.

Like The Flowers Need The Rain

Just like the flowers need the morning
dew is how my love longs for you.

I know you crave the same things too, but one
day, honey, it certainly will be soon.

I pray every night that God will see just how much
he needs to quicken your footsteps, so me you will
find, but while I wait I just thought you should know
this feeling that I hold on to I will never let go.

Just like all the flowers need the rain, when we find
each other we will relieve each other's pain.

Love

L- Loyal acts shown toward individuals. Learning to share intimate moments openly.

O- Open expressions of one's emotions held in dearest esteem towards a friend, child, or more importantly, a significant other.

V- Voluntary movements of the heart, and the vivacious perception felt by the actions taken whenever a deed of kindness is performed.

E- Engagement of your heart with fulfilling, exciting, warm, and passionate sensations that exudes from within.

Marinated and expressed well, love is all these ingredients. Love is a physical, spiritual, and emotional gesture, which gracefully arouses interest in the hearts of others!

Look Into My Eyes

Look into my eyes and tell me what you see. Is it just
a reflection of me? Or in these eyes do you see the
hungry thirst for someone wanting to be free?

Take another look and tell me again what
you see. Do you see the laughter trying to
unfold, which my heart seeks after?

If even for that very last chance I need you to glance and
tell me all of what you see when you look into my eyes.

Love Is Truly Being Able To Let Go!

Sometimes we love to the point where we stifle the other individual and we ourselves get stifled, not realizing that if we understand the true meaning of the word love, then we will be able to let go and allow love to manifest in our lives.

When you love you can allow yourself to free the other person physically and spiritually. At the time of letting go it will appear to be drastic and sometimes the most dramatic experience occurring in your life, but if you love—and not selfishly—free the one you love, and allow the rays to shine within them.

Thereafter you will eventually come to the realization that peace will surface within!

Marriage

M- Making a commitment to love.

A- Allowing each other the freedom of choice.

R- Respecting each other's opinions and decisions,
which are made for the betterment of the relationship.

R- Reassuring each other in hard times.

I- Inspiring each other in times of difficulty and despair.

A- Accepting each other's downfalls
and depleting them together.

G- Grace that you show to your love
ones in a gentle demeanor.

E- Enlighten each other when the other might not
quite understand something the way you do.

Marinated together well, these ingredients do
make a perfect and beautiful marriage among
two people who already love each other!

I Don't Want To Be An Obligation

Let me be a feeling that exists in the power
of a kiss—not an obligation to you at all—
creating settlement in your mind.

Please be there for only one thing, which is to allot
love in my empty spots, but if you ever feel that
somewhere else you should be, then go; don't feel you
need to take it easy with me. To me I need the truth,
which promotes me to abide in the trust booth.

Obligations are duties and tasks you see—not really putting
in all of your heart, because you feel that showing love
is like wearing a mask. Therefore, you can never elevate
me to the top, where my love needs to soar, creating
harmony inside and never allowing true love to hide.

No More Tears

Tears have fallen many times over, but the
well now feels dry from constant rigor.

My spirit feels so broken deep down inside; whether
my tears want to fall from me, they now hide. No
more teardrops do I have to fall. See, when you've cried
your whole life over there isn't much left inside.
I have conversations with my only true friend, and tell him
how broken my spirit is and how it needs so much to mend.
See, God is the only one I truly trust now, so I
empty my heart and ask him to sort it out!

Not Calling

Not calling doesn't mean I don't care, but faith
we must build in each other to survive allowing
this relationship to be full of pride.

I hope that when I'm absent you do no wrong,
but use this time given to fulfill our plan.

If for any reason this is not the case; then simply
this tells me I had made another mistake.

See, not calling certainly doesn't mean I gave up,
but instead to you I have entrusted my love.

When you hear from me I hope everything is okay,
because when we speak at times you make my day.

I do hope you feel the same way and see that
my not calling is time for you to breathe and
concentrate on the love we don't want to leave.

Over The Rainbow

Over the rainbow is where I really want to be,
exploring the magnificent colors, just you and me.

It's over the rainbow underneath the raindrop falls,
where we can cuddle the clouds into a sprawl.

Let us capture the rainbow before it's too late,
and into the skies our love can dissipate.

See, over the rainbow is where our love can be, if you'll be
brave enough to take this journey one more time with me.

People Needing People

Together we strive; we can achieve if only we unite.

People will always need other people, because
no man can stand alone. No man is an island,
but together we need a hand to rely on.

How can I help? Should I always ask? Am I the person who
will fulfill that task and assist you in your daily struggles,
or perhaps will I be the person to give the most hassle?

The world turns round and round, but without
each other that cycle will one day stop, so take a
step toward humanity not a false sense of security
asking "how" or "can it be me" to HELP!

Possessing The Will Power To Live!

In spite of popular belief, in order to possess the
abundance of life and wanting to live at your fullest,
the sole substance of willpower has to exist.
There are at times unfortunate circumstances that
occur in one's life, which create discouragement
in our hearts to continue living.
Sometimes it may be the dissolution of an
intimate relationship, which others see as
miniature, but you've held in great esteem.
At other times a physical illness may present itself,
and at this point your body, spirit, and soul are being
attacked, thereafter leaving you disconsolate toward
the joy of living. But even though these negative
circumstances will exist in life occasionally, once you
possess the willpower, you then have the essential
ingredient in life to conquer the opposing elements
which reign to distract you from the tranquil spirit of

life!

Sharing Is Caring

Share of yourself with someone less fortunate
than you; share of your time even though
to others that is worth a dime.

Care for someone when they are old, letting them
know they aren't alone in the cold, and to you
they can run for shelter whenever down, lending
your blanket of comfort and even sing a song.

Some people don't take the time to care, for to them
selfish they will always be, expecting only from you
and me, never to return the favor, if even just once.

Let us try to share and care for each other, because
only when you demonstrate these qualities will the
universe smile on you with its beauty and its peace.

Shining Star

Shining star, I see you no matter where you are.
Shining star, I see you no matter how far.
You gleam down from up above, hovering
over me with so much of your love!
I really didn't know that stars shine so bright until
the day you made your existence into my life.
One lonely night there I was, longing searching for a
reason to look up above. There they were— ever so bright,
again and again watching over me every single night.

Son

S- Sunshine that brighten each morning that I wake.
Sensitivity that you express towards my emotions daily.

O- Overconfidence that you show toward me
being able to conquer any obstacle. Outgoing
personality, which cheers me every day.

N- Newborn love that we develop for each other while
learning of each other's wants, needs, and personalities.

You're truly the reason I am who I am. You're why I
take on the battles that I do, knowing that you're my
guide there to take my hand through the storms.

Shattering of Trust

Many say trust can be repaired, but when a crystal, for
instance, falls and shatters; you then decide to mend
it by whatever means. Will it ever look the same?

Once trust becomes the betrayal of the heart,
the emotional, physical, and psychological
response usually won't be the same.

Trust must be surrounded by love, guarded
by respect, and entrapped by loyalty, because
those whose trust you have betrayed today the
universe will have you encounter tomorrow!

The Painting

How significant can one painting be? However,
this painting means the world to me.

Just like a mother that cradles her child; is
how I placed this painting in my arms.

From scratches and damage I made sure it did hide,
because a story was hidden way down inside.

I don't know if your value today is much, but
to my heart, you tenderly did touch.

You will travel with me throughout my life, because you
were there on my wall, watching me through the strife.

The Valley

In the valley is somewhere no one wants to be, but
this lonely place was a learning experience for me.

When you're in the valley, the mountains seems so
oversized and no longer do you have the faith to survive, but
the day will arrive for your experience again to come alive.

Just take this time to reacquaint with one self,
because this is a learning process you see and
clarity the valley will eventually reveal.

When the doors open again, then you can remember
the moment in the valley and be thankful to
be able to enter the doorway of elevation that
will have you no longer in isolation.

Not My Creation

Why does the world see beauty as such a
desirable thing; when to me a lot of sadness
and heartache it certainly did bring?

Beauty is not a creation that I sat down and invented, and
by all means, if this is how one is treated when possessing
this gift; I would try desperately to have it prevented.

Why don't we just learn to love what was created and extend
the part of each other that everyone was blessed with?

Everyone wants to alter themselves in some way, which tells
me they are dissatisfied with the way things were made.

Beauty doesn't just only exist from your external, but the
inner. Let us learn to capture the beauty that is within,
but only the patient will take time to see and explore
the other part of me; just waiting to set myself free.

The Zoo

There we were at the zoo to see the
animals run about so free.

Looking on from afar, some of the animals must wonder
why we come see them play and exhilarate so free.

Animals are caged; yet so free, like some
animals humans wish to be.

The humans live; yet the souls are caged, not allowing
them to get properly fed. No one locks them up at
night, but their souls constantly see no light.

Animals within a zoo get fed morning and probably at
noon. They know they have no job, but to be themselves
and walk about, unlike humans that work all day and
then their souls can't even be free at night to play.

Like animals some humans wish they were, to share no
care of this world; not only to walk the leash of life, but
to capture the moments thereafter without any strife.

Unity

U- Union in celebrating hearts, that can operate as one.

N- Never destroying the character of others and
needing to respect each person's achievements.

I- Integrity displayed amongst a large group, which
ignites peace and an orderly behavior between all.

T- Telling other persons of the attributes they possess and
the quality and rear-ness in which each one can be utilized.

Y- Yielding from negativity and transforming
to the yoke of togetherness, which leaves a
yearning in your hearts for less brokenness.

Uniting is the only way to let hope remain alive and bring
back the peace of positive vibes to exist in our lives.

TOGETHERNESS

Togetherness is one word with many syllables; just like
the world being one place with many different faces.
Togetherness brings everyone to become one, if we just
Unite and listen to the masters' plan.

Think of not only yourself everyday, but let someone
else know that you care; telling them by daily
expressions, or even a friendly call

No man's an Island can't you see? We all need each
other to give a hand, and keep the turning cycle of our
masters' plan.

One Plant Of The Same Tree

One plant that grows from the same
tree is what defines you and me.

Our thoughts are intertwined like the root that veins
into each vine; your heart is beating each beat of mine.

We see from each others eyes; making the
connection heavenly and divine.

Just like the leaf of a tree is how your
love penetrates life into me.

Each leaf receiving energy from the sun to grow and extend
the production plan to continue to decorate the land with
the blossom of new growth; allowing us to visualize our
future materialize in the cultivation of each others' eyes.